To:

From:

Date:

ZONDERVAN

The Weekly Prayer Project

Copyright © 2017 by Zondervan

Requests for information should be addressed to: Zondervan,
3900 Sparks Dr., SE, Grand Rapids, MI 49546

ISBN 978-0-310-08748-9

Cover design: Brand Navigation

Cover photography and illustration: Christine Errington

Interior design: Lori Lynch

Printed in China

19 20 21 22 23 24 / GRI / 16 15 14 13 12 11

THE WEEKLY Prayer Project

A Challenge to Journal, Pray, Reflect,
and Connect with God

Scarlet Hiltibidal

ZONDERVAN®

Contents

>>>>>><<<<<<

Lament

Intercession

Faith

Repentance

Awe

How to Use This Journal

Come and see what God has done;
he is awesome in his deeds toward the children of man.

Psalm 66:5 ESV

The journal you hold in your hands isn't just a pile of paper for recording random prayers, career goals, or calorie counts. It's a tool to help you intentionally, biblically, and joyfully quiet yourself so you can better hear God's still, small voice and connect with Him.

This book is divided into seven sections—each representing a different type of prayer found in the Bible, from prayers of gratitude and thankfulness to prayers of lament and intercession. Each week invites you to read from the Bible and then respond to the journaling prompts. These cues will challenge you to pray for yourself and others in specific ways that are modeled in Scripture.

Make this book your own! Start at the beginning, or jump ahead to the section that's most applicable to you. Each week you can look back at the insights you've recorded on previous pages, reflect on how God has shown Himself faithful, and explore the questions that still tug at your soul.

This year, be intentional in how you seek God and how often you seek Him. And share all His awesome deeds—the ones you read about in His written Word and in the words you write as you see Him work in your life.

Requests

Please, God

Maybe your dad was always there for you. Maybe he took you school-supply shopping, hugged you when you cried, and told that ex of yours that he or she messed with the wrong kid.

Or maybe your dad was deeply flawed. Maybe, through his words and actions or his silence and neglect, you learned that you'd better not ask him for anything. Or that you can ask all you want, but nothing's going to change.

This side of heaven, all parents have flaws. But if your perception of your heavenly Father is based solely on your earthly example, your view of God is skewed.

Your heavenly Father doesn't look at you and see the dishonest thing you did at work last year, the harsh word you said to your spouse last night, the thing you don't even want to think about that happened twenty years ago. When your Father looks at you, He sees His beloved, perfect child. Forgiven.

Because you are His child, nothing stands between you and Him. He wants you to talk to Him. He wants you to ask Him for things. He wants to bless you.

Philippians 4:6 urges you to "let your requests be made known to God" (ESV). Your prayers aren't useless. They aren't bouncing off the ceiling. They aren't being ignored. Your perfect Father happily hears, knows, and answers them because He loves you.

Just ask.

WEEK 1
Ask Confidently

>>>>>><<<<<<

*Let us then approach God's throne of grace with
confidence, so that we may receive mercy and
find grace to help us in our time of need.*

Hebrews 4:16 NIV

You don't need to be timid or self-conscious when you bring
your requests to God. The Bible says to approach Him with
confidence. You can walk before His throne confidently because
He has promised to help you when you need Him.

In the space below, write down the things that you
usually lack the confidence to ask or the things that
may seem too small to ask.

....

....

....

....

....

God wants an intimate relationship with you, and He loves to answer prayers specifically. List your prayer requests below.

....

....

....

....

....

....

....

....

....

....

....

....

WEEK 2
Don't Worry

>>>>>><<<<<<

*Do not be anxious about anything, but in every
situation, by prayer and petition, with thanksgiving,
present your requests to God. And the peace of God,
which transcends all understanding, will guard
your hearts and your minds in Christ Jesus.*

Philippians 4:6-7 NIV

Do you ever stay up late at night playing out scenarios in your
head? *If this happens, then that might happen, but then what if
that happens?* Rather than wasting a lot of time working yourself
into a spiral of stress, God wants you to cast your cares on Him.
Rather than planning for doomsday, tell God what's worrying
you. If you obey this command, He will give you peace.

What are you stressing over right now?

....

....

....

....

....

Look up Philippians 4:6–7 in another Bible translation, and write out the verses below. Read what you wrote out loud. Ask God to take away your burden and replace it with His peace.

....

....

....

....

....

....

....

....

....

....

....

WEEK 3

Nothing Is Impossible

>>>>>>>><<<<<<

At the usual time for offering the evening sacrifice,
Elijah the prophet walked up to the altar and prayed,
"O Lᴏʀᴅ, God of Abraham, Isaac, and Jacob, prove today
that you are God in Israel and that I am your servant."

1 Kings 18:36–37 NLT

The Old Testament prophet Elijah had an odd request for God, one that may have seemed impossible. Elijah wanted God to send down fire on a soaking-wet altar to show nonbelievers that He's real. God knows your heart. When you pray for something earnestly with the desire to glorify God, He loves to respond in miraculous ways.

In which seemingly impossible circumstances do you need God's divine intervention right now? List them.

....

....

....

....

As a reminder of God's faithfulness, list some times in your past when God has worked in seemingly impossible ways in your life, for your good and His glory.

···

···

···

···

···

···

···

···

···

···

···

···

WEEK 4
Up to God

>>>>>→←<<<<<

During that long period, the king of Egypt died. The Israelites groaned in their slavery and cried out, and their cry for help because of their slavery went up to God.

Exodus 2:23 NIV

The Israelites lived miserable lives as slaves. Given their circumstances, hopelessness was likely a common feeling. But they didn't just wallow in their pain. They cried out to God for help. They asked Him to help them, and the Bible says their prayers "went up to God."

Take some time to write your requests to God below. As you write them down, know and believe that your prayers are going up to God. He is listening.

I just ask that you help with sanity through these Covid times

God hears you, but He doesn't always answer immediately. Which prayers are you still waiting for God to answer?

Just continue to keep my family sane thru these times.

WEEK 5

Have Mercy

>>>>>⟫⟩⟨⟨⟨⟨⟨

*There were two blind men sitting by the roadside, and
when they heard that Jesus was passing by, they cried
out, "Lord, have mercy on us, Son of David!" The crowd
rebuked them, telling them to be silent, but they cried
out all the more, "Lord, have mercy on us, Son of David!"
And stopping, Jesus called them and said, "What do you
want me to do for you?" They said to him, "Lord, let our
eyes be opened." And Jesus in pity touched their eyes, and
immediately they recovered their sight and followed him.*

Matthew 20:30–34 ESV

Two blind men asked Jesus, God in the flesh, for mercy and
healing. And the Bible says that He took pity on them and
healed them. Isn't that amazing? When you are in pain, God
hurts with you. When you are sick and suffering, He is sad. He
cares. He heals.

List any physical ailments causing pain to you or
those close to you.

....

....

....

Ask for God's healing, knowing that He hurts with
you, cares for you, and still heals in miraculous
ways today.

....

....

....

....

....

....

....

....

....

....

....

....

WEEK 6
Finding Forgiveness

*"We deserve to die for our crimes, but this man
hasn't done anything wrong." Then he said,
"Jesus, remember me when you come into your
Kingdom." And Jesus replied, "I assure you,
today you will be with me in paradise."*

Luke 23:41–43 NLT

As Jesus hung on the cross, bleeding and dying for the sins of the world, a criminal being punished beside Him asked for salvation. And as Jesus suffered for that man's offense, Jesus said yes. No matter what you've done or where you've been, God longs to give you the freedom of His forgiveness.

Is there anything you can't seem to forgive yourself for? Are you struggling to forgive someone else?

....

....

....

....

When people hurt you, it can be hard to forgive them, even though Jesus offers them the same forgiveness He's offered you. Write a prayer asking God to help you let go of your anger and forgive someone who's hurt you.

....

....

....

....

....

....

....

....

....

....

....

WEEK 7
Wait Expectantly

꧁꧂

*In the morning, L*ORD*, you hear my voice;*
in the morning I lay my requests before you
and wait expectantly.

Psalm 5:3 NIV

Do you have any prayers you've grown tired of praying? God doesn't want you to pray just to hear yourself talk. He wants you to bring Him your requests and "wait expectantly." He wants you to believe that He is who He says He is—that He is powerful enough to do the impossible.

Think about your most longstanding prayers.
How has God changed your heart through those
situations?

....

....

....

....

....

In the space provided, ask God to do the impossible, and ask Him to help you to wait on His answer expectantly.

....

....

....

....

....

....

....

....

....

....

....

....

Thank You, God

We live in a shaky kingdom. There are bad guys and sinkholes and real-life natural disasters called "fire-nados," which are exactly what you think they are.

Because we live in this often volatile, always unpredictable world, we tend to focus on the earthquakes and the broken relationships and the mayonnaise-drenched sandwich we specifically and emphatically ordered with *no mayonnaise*.

The thing is, this kingdom full of unexpected pain and unwelcome condiments is not our home, and it's not forever.

Hebrews 12:28–29 says, "Since we are receiving a kingdom that cannot be shaken, let us be thankful, and so worship God acceptably with reverence and awe, for our 'God is a consuming fire'" (NIV).

We can be people who are overflowing with gratitude, even amid crummy circumstances, because our hope and joy don't depend on smooth sailing and sandwiches made to order.

When you pray, thank God for giving you everything you need and everything that matters. James 1:2–4 tells us to consider it "pure joy" (NIV) when we go through hard things because we know that God uses them for our good.

As God's child, you are receiving a kingdom that cannot be shaken. Whether you are stuck in the belly of a whale, a dead-end job, a painful marriage, or a difficult diagnosis, you can be thankful.

WEEK 8
Be Thankful

⊱⊱⊱⊱⊱⊰⊰⊰⊰⊰

Enter into His gates with thanksgiving,
And into His courts with praise.
Be thankful to Him, and bless His name.

Psalm 100:4 NKJV

What does it mean to enter the Lord's gates with thanksgiving and His courts with praise? When you pray, you are communicating with God. You are entering His courts. Beginning your prayers with gratitude puts your heart in the right posture.

How can you begin praying with a grateful heart?

....

....

....

....

....

....

Below, list three or four characteristics of God that stand out to you and why you're thankful for them.

....

....

....

....

....

....

....

....

....

....

....

....

WEEK 9
Child of God

>>>>>>><<<<<<

*Jesus declared, "I thank you, Father, Lord of heaven
and earth, that you have hidden these things from the
wise and understanding and revealed them to little
children; yes, Father, for such was your gracious will."*

Matthew 11:25-26 ESV

In these verses Jesus thanked God for revealing Himself to children. The faith required to believe that Jesus is God is a gift. No matter how old you are when you become a child of God, you are instantly made aware you are just that: a child, helpless to save yourself. And you know what? These verses show that God's grace is open and approachable for anyone.

In the space provided, write about the day Jesus saved you.

....

....

....

....

How can you thank God for giving you His most precious gift?

....

....

....

....

....

....

....

....

....

....

Sacrifice of Praise

>>>>>><<<<<<

But I will offer sacrifices to you with songs of praise,
and I will fulfill all my vows.
For my salvation comes from the LORD alone.

Jonah 2:9 NLT

To understand the magnitude of Jonah's prayer in this verse, you have to remember where he was. Jonah brought God songs of praise from within the belly of a whale. *A whale.* God is worthy of worship even when your circumstances are difficult.

Is there something that's keeping you from fully praising God?

....

....

....

....

....

....

Circumstances change, but God doesn't. You can praise Him for who He is, even when life feels overwhelming. What aspects of God do you need to rely on this week (Provider, Healer, Prince of Peace, and so forth)?

....

....

....

....

....

....

....

....

....

....

....

....

WEEK 11

Not Shaken

>>>>>>>><<<<<<

*Therefore, since we are receiving a kingdom
that cannot be shaken, let us be thankful, and
so worship God acceptably with reverence and
awe, for our "God is a consuming fire."*

Hebrews 12:28-29 NIV

You ou were created to live in God's perfect, eternal kingdom.
But you aren't just killing time here on earth, waiting for
God to make all things new. According to 2 Corinthians 5:17,
you're already new!

Which parts of your life are shaking your faith right
now?

....

....

....

....

....

List three things you can do this week that will matter in the eternal kingdom (love a neighbor, pray for a stranger, serve others, and the like).

WEEK 12
Joy in Community

>>>>>>><<<<<<

*We always thank God, the Father of our Lord
Jesus Christ, when we pray for you, since we
heard of your faith in Christ Jesus and of the
love that you have for all the saints.*

Colossians 1:3-4 ESV

In these verses, Paul and Timothy told their friends that they thank God for them in their prayers because of their faith in Christ. One of the most rewarding parts of being a Christian is having the hope and joy of community.

Who has God brought into your life to encourage you and support you? How can you be a better encouragement and support for them?

....

....

....

....

....

Write God a thank-you note for the godly people in your life. Thank God for the spiritual gifts you see in them.

....

....

....

....

....

....

....

....

....

....

....

....

WEEK 13

Worship

><<<<<<<<><>>>>>>>

Sing to the LORD with grateful praise;
make music to our God on the harp.

Psalm 147:7 NIV

Worship through song is something you find throughout the Bible. God loves when you're so overwhelmed by your gratitude that you praise Him through song.

List a few hymns or worship songs that are meaningful to you, and think about why those songs feed your spirit.

....

....

....

....

....

....

Write out some of your favorite lyrics.

WEEK 14
Rejoice Always

>>>>>≻✗≺≪≪≪

Rejoice always, pray without ceasing, give
thanks in all circumstances; for this is the
will of God in Christ Jesus for you.
1 Thessalonians 5:16–18 ESV

In these verses, Paul and Timothy wrote about giving thanks in *all* circumstances. If your happiness is based on things working out in your favor, you can expect to be disappointed. But if your hope is built on Jesus, you can find joy in the journey, even when life doesn't feel as smiley.

Write down a few difficult circumstances in your life. Then, below each one, write a reason you can find joy in it.

....

....

....

....

....

Search Scripture for promises about your future.
Write out a few verses that encourage you.

....

....

....

....

....

....

....

....

....

....

....

Why, God?

Maybe your overbearing boss or your always-there laundry pile or your smothering relationship is starting to feel just a little overwhelming. Okay, *a lot* overwhelming.

Or maybe it's something bigger. Maybe there's something that makes you want to go to sleep and never wake up. Maybe your body, your heart, or your dream feels broken.

All over the Bible, we read about people who suffered. Reluctant Moses tasked with leading God's jaded, whining, miserable people out of slavery. Job, who lost everything. David prayed through his depression. And then there's Paul, who struggled with what he called a "thorn in the flesh" (2 Corinthians 12:7 NKJV).

Self-inflicted pain. Bad-luck pain. Soul-betrayal pain. The pain of death. What pain.

But what a Savior.

Jesus, Son of God, knows every pain. He is the One we can turn to with our hurts, with our cries, with our laments. He's already proven on the cross how much He loves us.

When our circumstances are bad, God is still good. We don't have to say the right words to earn His favor. We have His favor already. His love for us is based on the good work of Jesus, not any feeble attempts of ours.

In our grief, anger, and discontent, when we sink into silence and despair, we can release our questions and laments onto the shoulders of a God strong enough to carry them. He will carry them. He will carry us.

WEEK 15
Troubled Soul

>>>>>><<<<<<

Let my prayer come before you;
incline your ear to my cry!
For my soul is full of troubles,
and my life draws near to Sheol.

Psalm 88:2–3 ESV

Sometimes life is so overwhelming that it can feel like the world is against you. In these moments, it may even feel like God Himself is against you. This psalm shows that when you're deeply troubled, you can tell God all about it. It won't change His affection for you in the slightest.

Do you find it difficult to share your hurts and hard feelings with God? Why or why not?

....

....

....

....

....

List three things that make you feel overwhelmed. Search Scripture and find three truths about God's character, then write those truths beside your burdens. Which seems bigger: the burdens or God's truth?

....

....

....

....

....

....

....

....

....

....

....

....

Run to God

I am disgusted with my life.
Let me complain freely.
My bitter soul must complain.
I will say to God, "Don't simply condemn me—
tell me the charge you are bringing against me."

Job 10:1-2 NLT

Job loathed his life. He lost everything. But He didn't run away from God. In fact, he ran to Him.

Have you ever gone through a season when you loathed your life? Did you run away from God or run toward Him?

....

....

....

....

....

If you ran from God, how do you think that affected your season of suffering? If you ran toward Him, write out all the ways He blessed and comforted you during that season.

....

....

....

....

....

....

....

....

....

....

....

....

WEEK 17
Turn to Joy

>>>>>×<<<<<

"Truly, truly, I say to you, you will weep and lament, but the world will rejoice. You will be sorrowful, but your sorrow will turn into joy."

John 16:20 ESV

As Christians, our lives aren't marked by perfect health and constant prosperity. In fact, Jesus promised that we *will* experience suffering. But with that promise of pain comes the hope that our sorrow will be turned to joy.

Write about a time you experienced deep pain but found joy and peace through Jesus.

....

....

....

....

....

....

If you are going through a season of suffering, write out a prayer of weeping and lament. Tell God you are hurting. Tell Him you are broken. If you don't know what to say, tell Him that. Rewrite this week's verse as a reminder that "your sorrow will turn into joy."

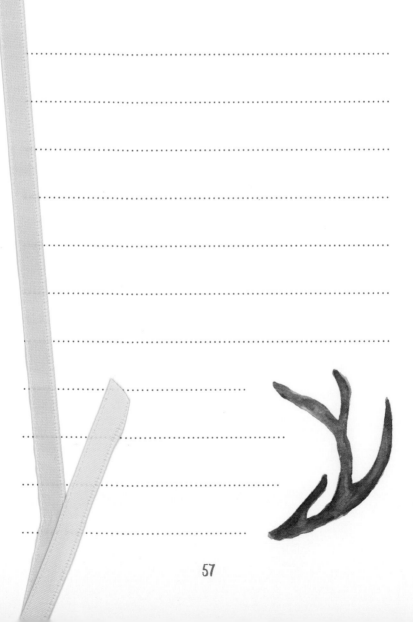

WEEK 18
Sufficient Grace

>>>>>><<<<<<

Lest I should be exalted above measure by the abundance
of the revelations, a thorn in the flesh was given to
me, a messenger of Satan to buffet me, lest I be exalted
above measure. Concerning this thing I pleaded with
the Lord three times that it might depart from me.
And He said to me, "My grace is sufficient for you, for
My strength is made perfect in weakness." Therefore
most gladly I will rather boast in my infirmities,
that the power of Christ may rest upon me.

2 Corinthians 12:7-9 NKJV

Whatever Paul's "thorn in the flesh" was—the Bible doesn't say—he begged for it to be taken away. He asked God for freedom. But when God's answer was no, Paul trusted that God had a purpose. He knew the sweet sufficiency of God's grace.

What are some areas of weakness in your life where you need God's strength?

....

....

....

Earnestly ask God for healing and help for the thorns in your life. Then entrust those cares to God. Remember, He has already proven at the cross that He is fully for your good.

....

....

....

....

....

....

....

....

....

....

....

WEEK 19
Too Heavy

✧✦✧✦✧✦✧

*And Moses said to the LORD, "Why are you treating me,
your servant, so harshly? Have mercy on me! What
did I do to deserve the burden of all these people? Did
I give birth to them? Did I bring them into the world?
Why did you tell me to carry them in my arms like a
mother carries a nursing baby? How can I carry them
to the land you swore to give their ancestors? Where
am I supposed to get meat for all these people? They
keep whining to me, saying, 'Give us meat to eat!'"*

Numbers 11:11-13 NLT

The Israelites were weeping, and their leader Moses was discouraged. He didn't slap on a smile and approach God with rehearsed or phony phrases. He was honest. He asked questions. He told God the burden was too heavy.

Tell God what you're carrying that feels too heavy.

....

....

....

Ask God to help you fully release it, fully trust that
He loves you, and walk forward with joy.

WEEK 20
God Answers

>>>>>><<<<<<

In my distress I called to the LORD,
and he answered me.

Psalm 120:1 ESV

God promised that He works all things—even bad things—together for good for those who love Him (Romans 8:28). So you can pray confidently, knowing that even if He doesn't "fix" your problems the way you want them to be fixed, He hears your prayers and answers in His perfect way. And God's way is perfect.

When you're in distress, it's easy to turn to the Lord for a quick fix. "God, please just fix it!" When have you prayed something like that? How did the situation turn out?

....

....

....

....

....

Write about a time when you called to the Lord in your distress and He answered.

....

....

....

....

....

....

....

....

....

....

....

....

WEEK 21
Supernatural Comfort

*"Blessed are those who mourn,
for they will be comforted."*

Matthew 5:4 NIV

No one can escape the heartache that comes with being human, but as God's child, you can rest assured that when you suffer, your Father will comfort you. That applies to the hurts this day will bring you; and more deeply, it applies to the mourning soul.

Write about a time when you felt God's supernatural comfort while you were mourning.

....

....

....

....

....

Are any of your friends or family members in a season of mourning? What are some practical, thoughtful ways you can comfort and support them?

....

....

....

....

....

....

....

....

....

....

....

....

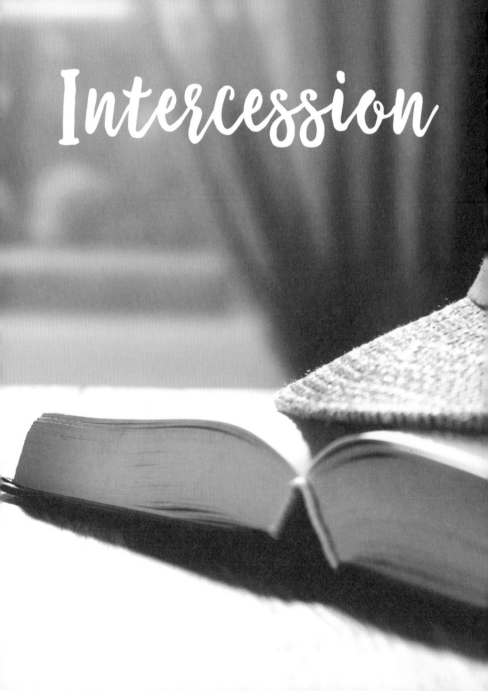

Intercession

Help, God

As Jesus was being crucified and suffering the physical, emotional, and spiritual punishment He didn't deserve, He prayed, "Father, forgive them, for they do not know what they are doing" (Luke 23:34 NIV).

Even in His death, Jesus was interceding for us.

And it didn't stop on the cross. After He defeated death and returned to the throne of the universe, He sent the Holy Spirit to intercede for us in our day-to-day lives.

The Holy Spirit even intercedes for us when we don't know how to intercede for ourselves. When we're too tired, too sad, too angry, or too confused, the Holy Spirit is interceding for us "with groanings that cannot be expressed in words" (Romans 8:26–27 NLT).

What a gift we have in the Holy Spirit.

And, as image bearers of Christ, we can intercede for others. We see it all over the Bible: Abraham interceded for Sodom. Moses interceded for the Israelites. Paul prayed for the church.

You can intercede for your boss. Or your estranged sibling. Or your unbelieving spouse.

James 5:16 tells us that our prayers have great power. We can ask God for healing and redemption in the lives of those around us. He'll listen.

We may not have the power to stop evil or prevent pain, but we have the ear of the God who does.

WEEK 22
No Words

>>>>>>><<<<<<

Likewise the Spirit helps us in our weakness.
For we do not know what to pray for as we
ought, but the Spirit himself intercedes for
us with groanings too deep for words.

Romans 8:26 ESV

What a wonder that the Holy Spirit intercedes for you, on your behalf, when you don't know what to say.

Do you ever struggle with knowing what to say to God? Do you worry you've been saying the wrong things? Or have you prayed with wrong motives?

....

....

....

....

....

....

Thank God for the gift of the Holy Spirit. Thank Him for knowing you so deeply and loving you so much that you don't have to say a word or think a thought to be known by your heavenly Father.

....

....

....

....

....

....

....

....

....

....

....

WEEK 23
Burden Bearer

>>>>><<<<<

Carry each other's burdens, and in this
way you will fulfill the law of Christ.
Galatians 6:2 NIV

In a world that tells you to look out for yourself and get ahead, Jesus' message of sacrificial love for others is a beautiful departure.

In what ways have others supported you during tough times? How did their help show you more of God's love?

....

....

....

....

....

....

Does someone in your life have an unmet need? How can you help this person? Ask the Holy Spirit for guidance.

....

....

....

....

....

....

....

....

....

....

....

....

WEEK 24
When People Pray

~~~~~~><~~~~~~

The men turned away and went toward Sodom, but Abraham remained standing before the LORD. Then Abraham approached him and said: "Will you sweep away the righteous with the wicked?" . . . Then he said, "May the Lord not be angry, but let me speak just once more. What if only ten can be found there?" He answered, "For the sake of ten, I will not destroy it."

Genesis 18:22–23, 32 NIV

Abraham begged God to save a wicked city if ten righteous people could be found there. And even though Abraham was the only one, God still said yes. This is one of many examples of God saying yes when people pray for others.

Write down four names of people you know and their specific situations. How would you like to see God work in their lives?

....

....

....

....

Commit to praying for these people every day this week. Then, if you see God answer that prayer, write down how He answered and put the date beside it.

....

....

....

....

....

....

....

....

....

....

....

....

Spiritual Wisdom

>>>>>>><<<<<<

I pray for you constantly, asking God, the glorious Father
of our Lord Jesus Christ, to give you spiritual wisdom and
insight so that you might grow in your knowledge of God. I
pray that your hearts will be flooded with light so that you
can understand the confident hope he has given to those
he called—his holy people who are his rich and glorious
inheritance. I also pray that you will understand the
incredible greatness of God's power for us who believe him.

Ephesians 1:16–19 NLT

In this passage, Paul asked God to give spiritual wisdom, and
he outlined what came with gaining that wisdom: knowing
the hope of salvation, the benefits of that salvation, and the
great power that comes with being a believer.

In what areas do you need to grow in spiritual wisdom
(studying the Bible with more intention, giving
generously, serving others, and so forth)?

....

....

....

Write out a prayer for the people of your church. Pray for the leaders by name, and ask God to give them wisdom. If you know your church staff has specific needs, pray for those too.

....

....

....

....

....

....

....

....

....

....

....

Praying Sacrificially

So Moses returned to the LORD and said, "Oh, what a terrible sin these people have committed. They have made gods of gold for themselves. But now, if you will only forgive their sin—but if not, erase my name from the record you have written!"

Exodus 32:31-32 NLT

Moses wasn't a perfect man, but his example was a beautiful foreshadowing of Christ. Moses asked God to forgive the sins of His people, even if it meant sacrificing himself.

How does this mirror the way that Jesus loves and forgives us?

....

....

....

....

Ask God to bring someone to your mind whom you can love sacrificially this week. Once you have a name and an idea, write it down and pray that God will give you the opportunity to serve that person this week.

....

....

....

....

....

....

....

....

....

....

....

Let Love Abound

>>>>>><<<<<<

This I pray, that your love may abound still more and more in knowledge and all discernment, that you may approve the things that are excellent, that you may be sincere and without offense till the day of Christ, being filled with the fruits of righteousness which are by Jesus Christ, to the glory and praise of God.

Philippians 1:9-11 NKJV

Paul prayed for the people at the church of Philippi that their love would abound and that they would be "filled with the fruits of righteousness" that come from Jesus.

What do you think being "filled with the fruits of righteousness" looks like? See Galatians 5:22-23 for some ideas.

....

....

....

....

....

Write a prayer asking God to make love abound in your community. Ask for God's grace in your own life and in the lives of those around you, that you would acknowledge all good works are really from Jesus.

....

....

....

....

....

....

....

....

....

....

....

....

WEEK 28

Confess and Pray

❯❯❯❯❯❯❯❮❮❮❮❮❮❮

Confess your sins to one another and pray for one another, that you may be healed. The prayer of a righteous person has great power as it is working.

James 5:16 ESV

When you confess your sins to someone, the Bible clearly says that you receive healing. Though confession isn't easy, and maybe you've been burned in the past, accountability helps you grow.

Do you live in community with other Christians where you feel close enough to confess sin and pray? If not, what's holding you back?

....

....

....

....

....

Have you been hurt in the past by people in your church or inner circle? What were the circumstances? Write out a prayer asking God to heal your heart, freeing you to live in closer community with others.

....

....

....

....

....

....

....

....

....

....

Are You Sure, God?

Faith.

Children have it. They believe what they're told. They believe fairies trade teeth for quarters. They believe kisses have the power to heal.

In Matthew 18:3, Jesus said that to enter the kingdom of heaven, we must become like little children. We must be people of faith.

As followers of Christ, we know that it takes faith to believe that Jesus is the Son of God, and it takes faith to trust Him, acknowledging that He is in control and we are not.

We love to be the ones behind the wheel of the car. The ones making the financial decisions. The ones who choose which matching pajamas to order for the family Christmas photos.

But God offers us the freedom of being like little children, following their good Daddy. And what a Father to have faith in! He really can trade our sorrows for joy. He truly does have the power to heal.

God loves to give to those who diligently seek Him. As we pray with faith, believing that He can answer, He *will* answer. And if we lack faith, we can just ask for more.

We have a loving, mighty Father in heaven who loves to show us what He can do.

WEEK 29

Trust in the LORD with all your heart,
And lean not on your own understanding;
In all your ways acknowledge Him,
And He shall direct your paths.

Proverbs 3:5-6 NKJV

These verses show you how to get the direction you need from God. Trust God with everything. Acknowledge Him in all your ways. Don't compartmentalize God and then come to Him in desperation when you have a situation you can't fix yourself.

What big decisions do you need to bring before God?

....

....

....

....

....

Try to identify an area of your life where God isn't as present as He should be. Is it at work? In your family? In the entertainment you consume? Write a prayer asking God to help you make Him a priority in every part of your life.

....

....

....

....

....

....

....

....

....

....

....

WEEK 30
Struggling with Doubt

[Jesus] said to Thomas, "Put your finger here; see my hands. Reach out your hand and put it into my side. Stop doubting and believe." Thomas said to him, "My Lord and my God!" Then Jesus told him, "Because you have seen me, you have believed; blessed are those who have not seen and yet have believed."

John 20:27-29 NIV

When you think about doubt in the Bible, Thomas is probably the person who comes to mind. In this passage, Thomas was struggling to believe that Jesus had been resurrected from the dead. Thomas wanted to see Jesus face-to-face and feel Him in the flesh.

In what ways do you see yourself in Thomas?

....

....

....

90

In the space provided, ask God to strengthen your faith today. Ask Him to help you have faith, even when He hasn't yet answered your prayers.

....

....

....

....

....

....

....

....

....

....

WEEK 31
He Listens

❯❯❯❯❯❯✕❮❮❮❮❮❮

Because he bends down to listen,
I will pray as long as I have breath.

Psalm 116:2 NLT

God isn't too busy for you. He doesn't listen to you half-heartedly or tune you out. He actively bends down to hear your prayers.

How does this verse change your perspective on prayer?

....

....

....

....

....

....

Tell God what's on your mind this week, and ask Him to work in each situation.

....

....

....

....

....

....

....

....

....

....

....

....

WEEK 32
Impossible Prayers

>>>>—>>>—<<<—<<<<

"For assuredly, I say to you, whoever says to this mountain, 'Be removed and be cast into the sea,' and does not doubt in his heart, but believes that those things he says will be done, he will have whatever he says. Therefore I say to you, whatever things you ask when you pray, believe that you receive them, and you will have them."

Mark 11:23-24 NKJV

God answers prayers. He did it for the first people He created, and He still does it today. He answers prayers about small, specific things, and He also answers impossible prayers. He's a good Father, working His perfect will in your life.

Write out the prayers that are on your heart this week, for yourself and for others. Then pray aloud, believing you have already received what you prayed for, even if you can't see those answers yet.

....

....

....

How has God answered your prayers in unexpected ways?

WEEK 33
Ask in Faith

*If any of you lacks wisdom, let him ask of God,
who gives to all liberally and without reproach,
and it will be given to him. But let him ask in
faith, with no doubting, for he who doubts is like a
wave of the sea driven and tossed by the wind.*

James 1:5–6 NKJV

Do you want to be wise? James 1:6 urges you to ask in faith, without doubting you'll receive that wisdom. This can be difficult for overthinking, overplanning, overanalyzing people like us. But God doesn't want an impressive spiritual vocabulary or a blameless record. He wants you to believe Him. And He wants your prayers to reflect that.

Ask God for increased faith and wisdom.

....

....

....

....

List the situations in your life where you want to be wise. Pray, believing that God will help you.

....

....

....

....

....

....

....

....

....

....

....

....

WEEK 34
Pour Out Your Heart

>>>>>×<<<<<

Trust in him at all times, you people;
pour out your hearts to him,
for God is our refuge.

Psalm 62:8 NIV

Trust in him at all times . . ." Not just sometimes. Not just when life is rosy and your friends like you and the reports at work make you look good. Trust Him when it looks like everything's falling apart—because He's still there beside you.

In the space below, do what this verse says and pour out your heart to Him.

....

....

....

....

....

....

In what ways can God be your refuge?

WEEK 35
Righteous Faith

>>>>>>>——<<<<<<

What does the Scripture say? "Abraham believed
God, and it was counted to him as righteousness."

Romans 4:3 ESV

God saw Abraham as righteous, not because he was a perfect man. In fact, the Bible is explicit about Abraham's many sins. So how did God see a sinful man as righteous? Because Abraham was a person of faith.

In the space below, ask God to help you walk through life this week, believing that He sees you as perfect and forgiven because of your faith in Jesus, not because of any righteous things you've done.

....

....

....

....

....

Think about the Christians in your life. Whose faith do you admire, and why?

....

....

....

....

....

....

....

....

....

....

....

....

WEEK 36
Help My Unbelief

〉〉〉〉〉✕〈〈〈〈〈

*Immediately the boy's father exclaimed, "I do
believe; help me overcome my unbelief!"*

Mark 9:24 NIV

This prayer is so honest. Are you ever afraid to tell God that your faith is weak? Do you ever pray, thinking, *This isn't really doing anything, but I know I'm supposed to do it?* God isn't a "supposed to" God. God is your Dad. He knows you're weak and that the human life is difficult and full of distractions. He knows you're broken and needy.

Below, be honest with God about your faith.

....

....

....

....

....

....

Are you enjoying a season of deep peace and assurance of your faith? Thank God for it below. Are you struggling to believe? Tell God, and ask Him to help you overcome your unbelief.

....

....

....

....

....

....

....

....

....

....

....

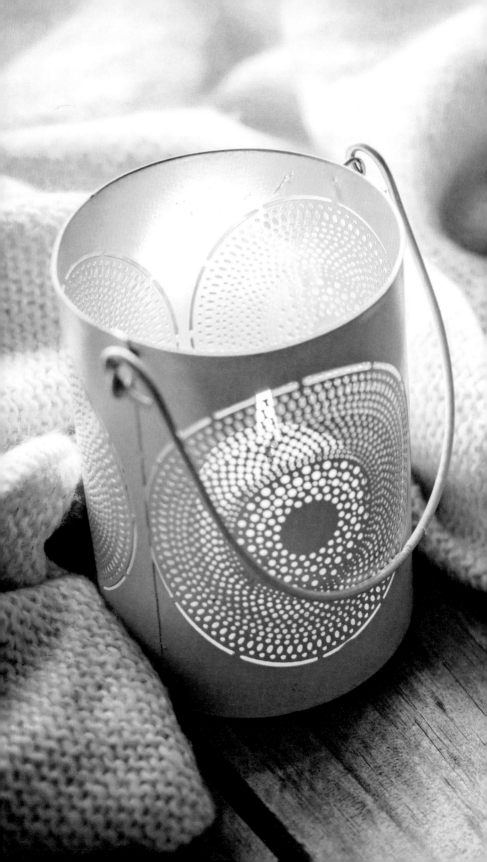

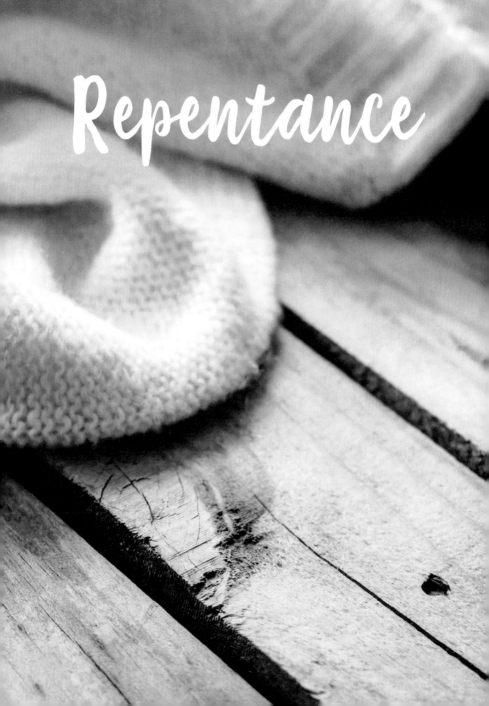

Repentance

I'm Sorry, God

Have you ever let someone off the hook with your mouth, while keeping them very much on the hook in your heart? It might have sounded a little bit like, "Oh, that's okay . . . water under the bridge." Cut to you speeding home, gritting your teeth.

Yeah. God doesn't forgive that way.

You've likely been on the other side of that too. You apologized, and the person you wronged went through the motions of restoration but held your shortcoming over your head for the longest time. Maybe they still do.

Yeah. God's people shouldn't forgive that way.

When we were so wrong, so guilty, so broken in our wrongdoing toward God, He reached down from heaven and offered us forgiveness. But not like the disingenuous, holding-it-over-your-head-until-the-end-of-time examples in our lives. Jesus takes our sin and removes it from us "as far as the east is from the west" (Psalm 103:12 ESV).

All He asks for is repentance. All He requires is a humble heart that says with sincerity, "I've wronged you. I need you. Please forgive me."

Repentance isn't needed *just* for salvation. It's needed every day. Confess the things you wish you hadn't said. Confess the things you wish you hadn't done. Confess the things you wish you *had* done. Confess that you're blind to some things. Ask the Lord to forgive you and help you turn again from your sin. Receive mercy from our good God who is "slow to anger and abounding in steadfast love" (Psalm 145:8 ESV).

WEEK 37
Gracious to Forgive

>>>>>—><—<<<<

*"Forgive us our debts,
As we forgive our debtors."*

Matthew 6:12 NKJV

This verse is part of the Lord's Prayer—Jesus' example of how to pray. This simple prayer of repentance requests that God make us, His children, as gracious to others as He is to us.

How has God been gracious to forgive you? Are there areas of your life in which you still need to ask for His forgiveness?

....

....

....

....

....

....

If someone has wronged you, write a prayer asking
God to help you forgive that person the way He does,
extending mercy and grace.

....

....

....

....

....

....

....

....

....

....

....

....

Please Forgive Me

>>>>⟩⟨⟨⟨⟨⟨

You said, "Listen and I will speak!
I have some questions for you,
and you must answer them."
I had only heard about you before,
but now I have seen you with my own eyes.
I take back everything I said,
and I sit in dust and ashes to show my repentance.

Job 42:4-6 NLT

In Job 42, Job owned up to sin, confessed to God, and asked forgiveness for what he did wrong. What changed Job's perspective? He saw his own sins in light of God's holiness.

How can focusing on God's holiness reveal areas of your life that you need to change?

....

....

....

....

When we confess our sin, turn from it, and turn to God, He blesses us. Below, write about a time you repented of specific sin and saw God's blessing as a result.

....

....

....

....

....

....

....

....

....

....

WEEK 39
No Regrets

>>>>>——<<<<<

*For godly sorrow produces repentance leading
to salvation, not to be regretted; but the
sorrow of the world produces death.*

2 Corinthians 7:10 NKJV

As a follower of God, your sins should cause you sadness and regret, but not lasting despair. Rather, your feelings should compel you to repent, to turn from the wrong you've done. This change ultimately leads to salvation.

How is godly sorrow different from the sorrow of a person who doesn't follow God?

....

....

....

....

....

....

Write your salvation story in the space below. If you've never recognized the sorrow your sin has brought to God and to yourself and your need to be rescued from it, write out a prayer of repentance below.

....

....

....

....

....

....

....

....

....

....

....

Washed Clean

>>>>>><<<<<<

Have mercy on me O God,
because of your unfailing love.
Because of your great compassion,
blot out the stain of my sins.
Wash me clean from my guilt.
Purify me from my sin.

Psalm 51:1–2 NLT

In this vivid example of repentance, the psalmist David asked for mercy. David exalted God's character. His love. His compassion. He asked the Lord to remove his guilt. He acknowledged his sin and that he deserved God's judgment.

In what ways should the posture of your heart resemble David's in this psalm?

....

....

....

....

In verse 12, David said, "Restore to me the joy of your salvation . . ." (NLT). Write about the joy you remember experiencing on the heels of true repentance.

....

....

....

....

....

....

....

....

....

WEEK 41

Return and Rest

>>>>>><<<<<<

This is what the Sovereign LORD,
the Holy One of Israel, says:
"Only in returning to me
and resting in me will you be saved.
In quietness and confidence is your strength."

Isaiah 30:15 NLT

I t's so easy to fall into a prideful pattern, thinking you have your life together. But God says your strength comes from returning to and resting in Him.

Do you ever find yourself treating spiritual rhythms, like spending time in prayer or reading God's Word, as demonstrations of your own righteousness?

....

....

....

....

....

In the space below, write what you think it looks like to live your life returning to and resting in the Lord. Confess whatever sin is keeping you from returning to and resting in Him.

....

....

....

....

....

....

....

....

....

....

....

....

WEEK 42
Promise Keeper

The Lord is not slow in keeping his promise,
as some understand slowness. Instead he
is patient with you, not wanting anyone to
perish, but everyone to come to repentance.

2 Peter 3:9 NIV

God wants you to repent because repentance restores your relationship with Him. Repentance trades your guilt and shame for unshakable joy and peace.

Do you tend to think of God as a patient, loving Shepherd who waits for His lost sheep, or do you tend to view Him as an angry, disappointed, oppressive Father? Describe your view of God.

Ask God to reveal His true nature to you. Search Scripture for descriptions of His character, and list any verses that stand out to you.

....

....

....

....

....

....

....

....

....

....

....

....

....

Forgive My Guilt

>>>>>><<<<<<

After he had taken the census, David's conscience
began to bother him. And he said to the LORD, "I
have sinned greatly by taking this census. Please
forgive my guilt, LORD, for doing this foolish thing."

2 Samuel 24:10 NLT

Living with unconfessed sin in your life causes overwhelming guilt, which can only be relieved by forgiveness from God—the only One with the power to pardon sin.

Is there anything eating away at you, leaving you with a guilty conscience?

....

....

....

....

....

....

You can live in a constant state of peace and freedom if your heart is in a posture of repentance—regularly confessing your sin to God, asking His forgiveness, and turning away from that sin. Write a letter of specific confession to the Lord, and ask for His forgiveness.

Good Fruit

❯❯❯❯❯❯❯❯❯❯❮❮❮❮❮❮❮❮

Bear fruits worthy of repentance.

Matthew 3:8 NKJV

In this verse John the Baptist was talking to the Pharisees, a group of religious people who thought they could rule-follow their way to salvation. John told them to bear fruits worthy of repentance. A repentant, humble heart is the only heart that can truly bear good fruit for the kingdom of God.

Do you feel pride when doing spiritual things, as if you have done well and deserve favor?

....

....

....

....

....

....

Write a prayer asking God to remove any pride in you and give you a repentant heart that can bear worthy fruit.

....

....

....

....

....

....

....

....

....

....

....

....

Awe

Wow, God!

Seriously? Did the car in front of you at Starbucks just pay for your latte and scone? Or maybe your boss just made you employee of the month and gave you a raise and a reserved parking space.

Many people spend their entire lives searching for the high of the *pinch-me* moments. Yet these moments, with or without scones, aren't truly *wow*-worthy.

But God is.

In a world bombarding you with miniature *wow* moments, it can be easy to misplace your worship and give your most awe-filled wows to the lesser things.

But you were created to worship God, so only when He has your heart can you find peace, joy, and contentment. The longer you linger in His Word and at His feet, the more awestruck you'll become.

Through Jesus, you have access to God. Through the Holy Spirit, you can talk to Him, even when you don't know what to say.

Jesus is *wow*-worthy.

And as His beloved, your hope is rooted in *His* wow. Your sin is forgiven because of *His* awesomeness. You will get a "well done," not because of any person you impress, title you hold, or amount of dollars you get to shuffle from one place to the other.

Wow.

WEEK 45
God's Splendor

꙳꙳꙳꙳꙳꙳꙳꙳꙳

Ascribe to the LORD the glory due his name;
worship the LORD in the splendor of his holiness.

Psalm 29:2 NIV

David wrote Psalm 29 as a song of worship for the Lord, poetically describing His incomparable power and His position on the throne, over all things.

Read the full psalm, and list the characteristics or names of God that mean the most to you.

....

....

....

....

....

....

....

When you pray, tell God how wonderful He is! In the space provided, use your own words to tell God everything you love about Him.

....

....

....

....

....

....

....

....

....

....

....

....

....

WEEK 46
Mighty Things

Mary said:
"My soul magnifies the Lord,
And my spirit has rejoiced in God my Savior.
For He has regarded the lowly state of His maidservant;
For behold, henceforth all generations will call me blessed.
For He who is mighty has done great things for me,
And holy is His name."

Luke 1:46-49 NKJV

Mary's response to the immaculate conception is striking. Rather than responding with fear or resistance, her prayer reflected an awestruck heart.

What about Mary's response is most surprising to you?

....

....

....

....

Make a list of the things, small or great, the Lord has done for you recently.

....

....

....

....

....

....

....

....

....

....

....

....

WEEK 47
In God's Care

>>>>>>⟩⟨⟨⟨⟨⟨⟨

Come, let us worship and bow down.
Let us kneel before the Lord our maker,
for he is our God.
We are the people he watches over,
the flock under his care.

Psalm 95:6-7 NLT

The language in this psalm is just bursting with the joy that comes from belonging to God.

What image do these words create in your mind? Describe or draw it.

....

....

....

....

....

....

Think about what it means to be someone God watches over, someone under His care. In the space below, make a list of things that trouble you. Then thank God for watching over you and keeping you in His care. Release your troubles, and trust that He loves you!

....

....

....

....

....

....

....

....

....

....

WEEK 48
Head and Heart

>>>>>⟩⟨⟨⟨⟨⟨⟨

"The hour is coming, and is now here, when the true worshipers will worship the Father in spirit and truth, for the Father is seeking such people to worship him. God is spirit, and those who worship him must worship in spirit and truth."

John 4:23-24 ESV

God doesn't want going-through-the-motions prayers. He wants true worshippers. He wants spirit and truth—your head and your heart.

Which do you struggle with more: your head or your heart?

....

....

....

....

....

Write out a few characteristics of God that you struggle to understand. Then, beneath that, write out parts of His character that are easier for you to grasp, and explain what He's done in your life that reveal those parts of His character. Ask God to help you worship in spirit and in truth.

....

....

....

....

....

....

....

....

....

....

....

WEEK 49
Praise Him Anyway

Is anyone among you in trouble? Let them pray. Is anyone happy? Let them sing songs of praise.

James 5:13 NIV

God wants you to pray to Him when you're suffering *and* when you haven't a care in the world. When things are going well, it's easy to forget the Father. But James said to sing praise in our cheerfulness.

In the space below, take time to worship God for everything He is, whether things are cheery or life feels like it's crumbling beneath you.

....

....

....

....

....

....

Feelings and circumstances change. God doesn't. Tell God thanks for being your constant, and make a list of ten reasons why He is worthy of praise.

....

....

....

....

....

....

....

....

....

....

....

....

WEEK 50

Come See

Come and see what God has done:
he is awesome in his deeds toward the children of man.

Psalm 66:5 ESV

In these verses, the psalmist praised God for His awesome deeds and invited others to come see.

Make a list of five blessings from God, whether you realized they were blessings at the time or not. Read over your list, and take comfort in the fact that the Lord is still at work.

....

....

....

....

....

....

Consider sharing this list with someone as an encouragement and a reminder that God is glorious and His deeds are awesome.

....

....

....

....

....

....

....

....

....

....

....

....

....

WEEK 51
God's Fame

>>>>>>*<<<<<<

LORD, I have heard of your fame;
I stand in awe of your deeds, LORD.
Repeat them in our day,
in our time make them known;
in wrath remember mercy.

Habakkuk 3:2 NIV

In chapter three, Habakkuk spoke of God's wrath and anger toward the wicked. His circumstances were not fluffy or peaceful. He anticipated catastrophe. But in verse 18, he prayed, "Yet I will rejoice in the LORD. I will be joyful" (NIV). When life looks scary, you can worship God because He is your strength.

Write down two circumstances in your world that feel scary.

....

....

....

....

Describe some ways God has used scary circumstances to draw you closer to Him.

....

....

....

....

....

....

....

....

....

....

....

....

Faithful and True

>>>>>>><<<<<<

I saw heaven standing open and there before me
was a white horse, whose rider is called Faithful
and True. With justice he judges and wages war.
His eyes are like blazing fire, and on his head are
many crowns. He has a name written on him that
no one knows but he himself. He is dressed in a robe
dipped in blood, and his name is the Word of God.

Revelation 19:11-13 NIV

In the first half of Revelation 19, we see the Lord being worshipped in heaven. Then, beginning in verse 11, we get to read a vivid description of His return. Mighty. Powerful. Our Savior, returned! Wow. This is the One we worship.

Search your heart and, in the space provided, write out some of the phrases that grab your attention in this passage.

....

....

....

Write about any aspects of your life that are not revolving around the One who is called Faithful and True. Ask God to shift your focus back to Him—the only One who is truly worthy of your wow.

....

....

....

....

....

....

....

....

....

....

....

....